The Interview: Preparing for, Surviving, and Life After. The Handbook for Mastering Your Interview Experience

by

Jesse Turner, MBA

The Interview: Preparing for, Surviving, and Life After. The Handbook for Mastering Your Interview Experience

ISBN- 9781686235856

Copyright ©2019 by Jesse Turner

All rights reserved. No portion of this book may be copied, re-transmitted, reposted, duplicated, or otherwise used without express written approval of the author, except by reviewers who may quote brief excerpts in connection with a review. Any unauthorized copying, reproduction, translation, or distribution of any part of this material without permission by the author is prohibited and against the law.

Printed in the United States.

First Printing 2019

An application to register this book for cataloging has been submitted to the Library of Congress.

**Dedicated and In Memory of my brother
Emery Karon Williams**

*For all the times we dreamed and planned to
"Get it All!"*

Table of Contents

Introduction 1

Chapter 1 Why are you Looking? 5

Chapter 2 The Five Deciders 10

Chapter 3 Recognizing the Opportunity for Career Growth 28

Chapter 4 Preparing for the Big Day 36

Chapter 5 During the Interview 50

Chapter 6 Surviving 60

Chapter 7 You got the Job! 75

Chapter 8 Life After 78

Chapter 9 Conclusion 84

Introduction

As a professional in the finance industry, banking specifically for more than 2 decades; I've had the pleasure to work in various roles. Those roles included being in a front-line clerical position, team lead position, front-line supervisor position, management, and different senior management roles. Reflecting on those years of experience remind me how I got to my current career status. Simply put, not until about 7 years ago did, I take control of my own career. With humble beginnings of working my way up and through banking operations on into management; I can clearly remember the day when I knew that I reached a ceiling. At that point, I took the initiative to complete my post-secondary education to surpass that ceiling, only to bump my head into a new ceiling. The ceiling that I speak of was conquered by mastering the interview process. What I mean by mastering the interview process is realizing that I had to stay true to myself, be able to speak to real-world work experience, and project confidence without arrogance.

There are revelations and steps to be able to fully understand how to interview, why to interview, and when to interview. This handbook will provide you the basic tools to be able to take a step back, evaluate yourself, and your position in your own career-path goals. Just as preparing for an interview takes interpretation of the position needs in relation to your experience; your interpretation of this handbook is what will enable you to be able to master interviews. This handbook will not provide you with a magic pill, or industry secrets to win every interview. What it will do is provide you with information that you can digest, interpret, and apply to your own interview style.

Going back to that ceiling I was able to surpass twice and those last seven years of my career of taking control of my own destiny; a light went off. Once the light went off, I was able to do the following: Survive an organizational merger between two banks, one of which I had been with for almost 14 years. I was able to put myself in position to be retained when meeting the new management of the new organization and win them over. With that, I found a new career path in the new organization, interviewing internally and successfully getting the new position offer. A year later; I was able to interview outside of my organization, get the job offer; but turn it down to stay with my organization. Not too much later after that, I got another interview externally, won the interview, but also turned it down to stay. Yet another external interview months later, won the interview; and finally got the mindset to leave my long-time standing with the organization I called home. A year later, I began to connect with fantastic recruiter, and became curious about an opportunity to help build an organization's Treasury Management function. I won the interview and took a position that called for me to build out that department for an organization. Of course, the obvious question will come up; why would you interview and entertain so many different jobs/positions? This handbook will address that, and why in some individuals case, it enhances professional development.

Hopefully, you'll take this handbook, read it, interpret it, and use the teachings, advice and coaching to mold your own story to climb passed your own career ceilings. I have an extraordinary passion to share knowledge, help others, and enjoy witnessing the success of everyone around me. Of course, there are other books, tools, and advisors in the world that can give advice on interviewing. This handbook is based on real-world experience, knowledge, receiving mentorship, mentoring others, and will possibly serve as a tool to allow me to spread the possibility of career success on to others to the point that I can witness an unlimited number of professionals succeed!

Enjoy!

Jesse Turner MBA

Chapter 1   Why are you Looking?

Anytime you begin to look for another job, position, or career; it is of the upmost importance to always ask yourself why! Seems so simple, yet be it getting caught up in the emotions of a couple bad days, horrible projects, work assignments, bad management, not so friendly co-workers; we've all found ourselves in the application purgatory. That moment when you are fed up after a long-days' work and begin applying for any and every position that just barely comes close to your experience. That is, until you run out of the stamina to continue to go through the 15 page, 30 minute on-line process on a website to give your background to a hiring system, linked to a recruiter or an H.R. representative's email address, whom most likely will overlook your talent for the next individual. After all that work!! Therefore, asking yourself why is highly important. I don't mean just briefly asking yourself in your head as you stand on the company elevator waiting for your floor. I don't mean just asking yourself why while you wait for the kids to get out of the car in the morning while you drop them off at school. Even the few minutes you spend in the bathroom brushing your teeth at night or in the morning while you prepare for bed or that job you no longer like.

Asking yourself why you are applying for another job or position simply means sitting down and taking out a piece of paper, the old-fashion way. This is important because we must be able to take inventory. Inventory of our own self. A list, or multiple lists. What is your motivation? What is making you not like the job? Are there any positives left in the position you currently hold? All of this is important because sometimes, when we feel we've had enough, we only see the negative. On purpose! What I mean by this is that when we want so badly to obtain a new opportunity, we tend to start to feel like everything and everyone is against us. Even the small good things get turned into a negative some-how. This is something that must be avoided. How do we avoid this? A list. Good-ole pros-cons list. We must take the time to outline the benefit and the disadvantages of leaving our current position. Very simply put; the benefits list could be minimal benefits. This is fine! Why, because sometimes the small benefits will make the difference between a good decision to move on, or a horrible choice to jump out there into the world. Some examples of benefits are; maybe the lunchroom serves good healthy food at a good price. Maybe your pay is not where you want it, but your commute is close to home. Maybe the manager is not that good of a manager, but you love your co-workers like family. All of these are examples of positive benefits that can possibly be the deciding factor in even looking at all. But of course; we must put together that bad list. It must happen! I am sure that I don't have to give examples of a bad list for a job. But one must be careful to do the following when making a list of the bad things at your job that would motivate you to look. Once the "bad" list is complete; review it, review it, and review it! Why so much? Look at each item on the "bad" list and rank them – top to bottom. Now look at the last 3 -5 items. Chances are those last few items on the list can be on the border of good/bad. Can possibly be taken off the "bad" list all together? Am I correct? I've found this to be true with many people that I've mentored over the years. These items either end up on the good list or get removed. Now that we have both lists, we compare. Which list has more is the first step?

Scenario 1: If your "bad" list still has more, take heed of the top 3 and make sure that those three items are indeed game changers that absolutely would make you happy if you could improve them. Now look at your good list. Take the top 3 from that list. Are these three items available anywhere? At any organization? Or can they only be obtained where you currently work? This is important because if they are only offered by your employer; that equates to 2 benefits! It is an un-fair advantage that your currently employer may possibly win against any other company. If you can only get these items from just your employer; then maybe your situation is not so bad? Examples of a "good" list of items that your current employer gives, and you may not be able to obtain elsewhere are a sabbatical, or a pension. Now we are talking about a "good" list that produced some positive items that are contributing to your overall mental health and post-work health. We must be very careful to not give up too much for the immediate satisfaction of a new start.

Scenario 2: If your "good" list already has far more items than your "bad" list; you are in need of some real look-in-the-mirror evaluation. Quite simple, if you can put together a large list of positive items about the job you are trying to leave; there may be a couple things happening here:

1 – You have far too much experience for the job you are doing, and now it is mundane

2 – You desperately need a change of scenery, so now you look for the same or similar position with even more perks.

With both scenarios and lists, you now have a good base to ultimately decide if a move is right for you in this moment in your career.

Chapter 2   The Five Deciders

Now let's get into the "why" a bit deeper. Now that we've created pros and cons lists. Evaluated those two lists, and possibly looked within ourselves. Let's dig in! I want to dedicate this chapter to what I like to call "The Five Deciders". What are the five deciders? These are five items; reasons that should apply to any person, any job, any career, any situation; and make the overall decision for you if it's time to move on. Basically, picking up and changing careers or jobs, or even positions in the same organization takes a lot of thought. We must weigh everything! In most cases, the decision has far more to do with than just yourself. You may have a family. You may have kids; you may be a person that cares for your parents. Those family and friend factors may keep you from taking a new role. Especially if the role is in a new city. We must be calculating and measured in the decision. Of course; if you are making a poor salary, and working for a bad manager, and driving for what seems like forever on your commute! Just make the change! You'll save yourself a lot of heartache for sure!

Let's talk about the cases when the lines are somewhat blurred. Cases when you are in a decent spot at your current job, not the best. The new potential job has a bit more perks, maybe a little more money. However; when you really think about it, you don't know if it will truly make you happy to make a move. This is when you must apply the deciders. The deciders coupled with following your heart and mind, with a little advice form only the people you truly, deeply trust will allow you to make a well thought out decision to take the leap and put yourself out there. To kill the suspense; let's get into exactly what the "Five Deciders" are:

- Number one is pay
- Second comes duties/job description/job type
- Third we have work environment
- Four is commute
- Number 5 and the last of the deciders is level of happiness

These are the five basic needs to help you decide if you are in a good position currently. They will help you decide if you are just getting up every morning at 5am to just pay the bills, or if you like your job or career. Believe it or not, these five factors will help you decide if you can ever use the "L" word when talking about your job. Trust me, I've only been able to use the "L" word twice in my long tenure of working. This should be the goal; to be able to say, "I Love My Job!" We all must go through some growing pains. We all at some point find ourselves on the climb of a ladder with an organization. We've all had to grind at some point. Work extra early, or work extra late, and on weekends. What matters is if it is all worth it in the end. I am telling you right now! Being born in the late 70's, and growing up in the 80's, and watching the "Baby Boomers" generation stay faithful to companies until their mid-60's, then retire with sometimes a pension or just social security and any retirement money to still struggle?? We must take control and put ourselves in position to be able to sit back at some desk, somewhere, at some point in our career, and say' "I Love My Job!" The five deciders will help us make measured decisions as we move along the path of our career through the years. Therefore; we must really take the time to evaluate every potential opportunity and break down each decider.

So, what about pay? Well, pay is and should be the most important factor! I am sorry, anyone who tells you money is not important is either a fool, has a lot of money already, or was educated early about debt, or put in a position to not have any debt as an adult. Okay, okay, I get it! Calling someone a fool is a bit extreme! I won't take it back, but I will expound on my statement. It is possible to not make money the priority early in your career. How? Maybe you want experience, so you intern. But why do you intern? To try to impress an organization to get hired full-time or referred to get hired. Or to use that company as a good reference to get hired with another organization. Another way that money could not be as important at first, is if you have a means to be able to find your way, because your parents are doing well financially. This is the way I've raised my children. I've told each of my children to make sure that they find what they love first, then get the money after. This is because I chased money early in my adulthood, only to find what I love later in my 30's. Very frustrating! But let's not take our eyes off the prize here. Even if you have reasons, means, or just desire to not make money the focus at first, eventually you will. To put it simple, our world, way of life, cost of living; should I continue? All of this and more will eventually make you have to raise your income. If for nothing else, to make sure you can retire in a respectable financial standing.

When looking at potential jobs, you always want to look at the pay for the position. In most cases, a job site will list the estimated salary for the position. If the estimated salary is not listed with the position, there is another way to find at least a close comparison to the salary. Take the position title and do a web search on that title. In this age of information overload, you are guaranteed to find a web blog, website, or job site that has that exact title or similar with some sort of salary history. The specifics of pay and negotiating pay after you've passed an interview, we'll get into later, but you want to always look for a new position that gives you a decent raise. If not, then you'll want to balance it out and do the calculations of your commute cost versus the pay. It may be possible that you take a slight pay cut for other benefits but find that cutting your commute costs give you a raise. In the end, just make sure you always go for more pay when venturing out. Even if the job only estimates what you get paid right now; if you can master the interview, you'll be able to negotiate more, if they really want you! Oh, that's right; isn't that why we are here? Reading this handbook!?! Indeed!

What about those duties/job description/job type? Very important to say the least! To introduce this decider, let's take a trip to our past. Let's think back to when we were just little kids. Hanging out with your friends on your neighborhood block, in a lunchroom sitting at a lunchroom table, sitting in your backyard with your cousins. Are you starting to remember the moment? The conversation between the two of you, or group of you? The oh so familiar conversation that goes a little something like this; "I want to be a _____ when I grow up!" Now look at that statement. The blank underline; let's fill it in. What do we put in the blank underline? Right; a job description, don't we!? We wouldn't put a dollar figure there, would we? We wouldn't put a destination there, would we? We wouldn't put "a cool co-worker/employee" in that blank underline, would we? No, we would not. That blank underline will always be filled with a title. Such as, Police, Doctor, Nurse, Lawyer, basketball player, dentist, and so on… Therefore; even if your path leads you into the finance, or manufacturing, or the sales world, we still need to fill that blank underline in eventually. This is where the second decider becomes so important. That job duty/job description/job type is a decider. You absolutely must like what you do. If you don't like what you do; you need to get to work anyway! The main factor of all the five deciders will always balance out, if you can be happy with what you do. As a matter of fact! Each of the deciders will lead to happiness and less stress. Therefore; we must take the necessary steps to ensure that we like our duties after we master that interview, successfully negotiate that favorable salary, and take that new position. Everyone loves to do something, but realistically; we cannot always do what we love as our primary source of income. But we can come as close to it as we can to making our job become enjoyable. There is a difference, but we all know that we can live daily having something we love, and something we enjoy. Using both to balance our overall life and happiness. Examples of this is I love to garden in my backyard. But I enjoy managing projects. Yes, I suppose I could start a landscaping company and build it up to have many employees and clients to make money for what I love. However; I have found that I can make a lot, sometimes a boatload of money managing projects for a company! See how that goes? Then we must make sure that we search, apply, and get positions that are conducive to being able to like our duties/job description/job type. Trust me, it will benefit you in ways that are un-measured.

The work environment will judge every single day of your life. So, by now; you know how to decide why you want to make a change. You know how to ensure you apply for positions that will pay you right. You've discovered how to make sure you search for organizations that will give you duties you like to do, or maybe even love to do. What about the work environment? There is no way for you to truly know this until you accept the position and get to your new desk or office. Until you get that first weird stare from your new co-workers. Until you get that first ridiculous email from someone in the organization asking you for something that you could not possible give on your first day or week! This is when you must look at your current work environment. This is what I like to call "going out on the balcony" and looking at your whole picture. Is your current work environment the perfect environment? If you are looking, it is quite possible you have already answered this question. But in some cases, it is not that simple. Since we cannot know about a work environment, unless we know someone who works for our next employer, we must look at our current situation to have a measuring stick.

Let's take some time to evaluate where we stand right this moment, at our current employer. Are your co-workers only co-workers? Do you engage in any out of work relationships with your co-workers? How is the relationship with your manager? How comfortable is your workspace? Do you feel empowered in your position? Do you feel the environment is inclusive? Just some questions to get started measuring your situation. So, let's take some time to go through the questions. Co-workers being friends or closer is important to judging your work environment. If you rarely communicate with co-workers other than for work assignments; something could be amiss. If you never attend after-work events, there is a reason for that. Building relationships; friendly and professional play a role in enjoying your work environment. Even if you don't feel it necessary to get all cozy with co-workers, entertaining a healthy relationship helps you feel good about the work environment. Therefore; if you cannot even muster the energy to establish building good relationships at all, you are in the wrong environment.

Ah the manager/employee relationship; this relationship can go in so many directions. Once you figure out the type of manager you have, then you must figure out if that personality type meshes with your own personality and professional mentality. This is where lines can become blurred. Since we tend to blame everything that is wrong on management because management has the responsibility of over-seeing. This is simply not a fair act, yet we all do it at times. As professionals, we must take accountability to the work environment just as the manager. In some cases, even more than the manager. Once we can figure out the type of manager we have; if we can co-exist and if the relationship can grow, only then can we fully determine if the management/employee relationship caters to our own needs of enjoying the environment. At this point, if for any reason, we see that it may not work, we must evaluate ourselves and ask if we are the root of the issue of the relationship with the manager. Then, and only then can we truly be unbiased at making the decision of how the relationship goes into the future with this manager. But make no mistake about it! It's not all on you either! If you are honestly nurturing the relationship with your manager, and they seem okay, but you still cannot answer if the relationship feeds a healthy work environment, then make the following questions list about the manager:

- Does the manager communicate with you?
- Does the manager respect you as an adult professional?
- Does the manager encourage career growth?
- Does the manager critique you for the purpose of professional development?

- Does the manager treat every employee equally within reason?
- Does the manager promote ambition, drive, and professional gains?

It is my belief that we must hit on at least four of these questions, with the respect one being THE most important! Of course, no manager is perfect. At times, a manager may be in the process of learning to be a manager; therefore, it is okay for them to be lacking on some of these questions. But that is where you come in as a professional in your role to nurture the relationship, and you both grow together as the environment continually improves.

Where you are setup in your organization matters! Do you have a desk, cubicle, office, or share bench seating because you get to be remote quite often? Going to a building 5 to 6 days a week for 8 – 10 hours a day can be demoralizing! Therefore; we must take note on if we are truly comfortable in our workspace. You may not desire an office or cubicle, but you must be able to possibly make this space a second home. Why? Think about the 5 to 6 days a week for 8 – 10 hours that we just mentioned. That's why! Adding that up can become more time spent than with your family and friends. So, we must be able to answer the question of if we are truly comfortable in the workspace. Without that comfortability, we lose on the loving the environment aspect, even with other factors being aligned perfectly!

How about empowerment? Does your job or manager enable you to make decisions in your role? This can become very important in a career. Why? Because of the mundane factor. If you feel that you are stuck in a rut, are unable to give any input daily, that can begin to feel like disrespect. One fact about the human being is, we love to be opinionated. If our ideas are caged, we lose the passion for any task or situation. Therefore, think about if your manager or position allows you to have input, or take ownership for some duties in your workweek? If so, then you may find that your standing in the environment is not so bad.

The feeling of inclusiveness matters as well. Simply think about any large group of people doing anything. If the group is standing around, there will most likely be a circle, or semi-circle forming. If you are standing on the outskirts of that circle, then you are not feeling the inclusiveness. This can happen in a work environment also. The management and co-worker situation must give you the confidence that you are not always the last to know every bit of news or change. If this begins to happen, you have some real evaluating to do, and you need to be looking for a new opportunity anyway. I say this because, if you are being left out all the time, one of two are happening. One, you are being discriminated against for some reason. Two, you are the problem, and everyone wants to avoid conflict with you. Either way, you are not fitting in to that environment, and need to search for an environment that better suites you.

Driving for hours on end will make you want to scream and pull your hair out. I have personal experience with this. At times, the thought of making exactly the amount of money you've always wanted will make you think that it doesn't matter how far of a commute you make daily. However; long commutes can drain you mentally, physically, and emotionally. Therefore, the commute is one of the critical deciders. The commute will play a crucial role in your interview process as well. Just knowing that a potential job or organization is a little too far for you to commute everyday will disrupt your interview preparation. Putting yourself in the position of receiving an interview with a company that seems to be a great organization, offering a great position, and the potential to earn a good salary; but it is just inside of relocation regarding distance from home. There is a strong possibility that the commute will be the most prevalent topic on your mind. Thus, leaving you in a position to spend far too much brain power on the commute than the actual interview process. In comes the distraction that grows as you inch closer to the interview date. Why? Because if you really think that you may accept the offer, if presented, you will begin to mentally try to justify sitting in a car for hours, or getting on multiple trains, and buses to get there. Next you will begin to verbally justify those same reasons to everyone around you that may question your thinking in even taking an interview so far from home.

With the default justification beginning to brew, you will unknowingly begin to do the following three things; constantly think about the potential of pay at this position, build the position up to be your "dream job" when it may not actually be that; and lastly, under prepare for the interview due to the self-convincing you will do to justify the distance. Simply put, as we get more experience, more talent, and more value in the market; we must make sure that the commute is not taxing. If we find the commute taxing on our body and mind, then it is not worth it. Of course, I am fully aware that there are situations that arise when you need to take the job no matter what; even if the commute is a small road trip. However; this is where the experience, talent, and market value come into play.

We must understand our value in the market in order to avoid the commute dilemma from the start. Value Yourself! Period! There is a reason you work hard, earn experience, gain more education. To be able to pick and choose where you work, how you work, and when you work. Currently, because of technology we can use negotiation as a tool for more than just salary and vacation days. The aspect of working remote can be a strong bargaining tool. A tool we must not be afraid to use. This brings us full circle to the start of this topic, the topic of commute. You've found a great organization, the position you found is something you want to do, and would do well, you know that you have the where withal to be able to win the interview, but; sigh! It is 65 miles away from your home! Your interview preparation must include displaying examples, and proof of your experience working, managing projects, and communicating efficiently and effectively via web meetings, phone, and email. This is very important because you want the hiring manager to walk away with two main beliefs about you. That you are really the best candidate to hire, and that you will not have to be monitored on any project that is assigned to you as an employee. Then the commute dilemma can be solved. In cases such as being pegged as an absolute "Have to Hire" candidate, interviewing in a manner that proves your worth no matter where you work will erase any anxiety about commute, or possibly even relocation.

Ah Happiness! How do we truly measure happiness? Well, your level of happiness will be driven by the previous four deciders. But there's a bit more to it to achieve true happiness. Let's think about what we discussed back when we talked about finding something to like, then getting money and vice-versa. At my now mature age; when speaking to my children, giving advice and tools for the future, I always tell them to find something they love to do first! Of course, I have built a decent foundation at home to allow them to be able to go out into the world to "find themselves" before they just jump into the real-work world. But finding what you really love to do is very important. There will become a point in your career where you will find that liking what you do is way at the top of the list. Basically, when we are young; typically, money is always first. Then we may say location, or profession. But as we get older and wiser, the list starts to turn upside down. Each year working that goes by, we begin to value the opposite as high priority. For example; at 23 years old, you may feel that you need to make as much money as possible, and that may be the focus. By 29 – 30; you start to value other important factors, such as work hours and commute. When you get to 40 years old or older; then just simply liking the job becomes priority.

I want my children, and anyone else in the world I can influence to try their best to find what you love first. Then the money will come! Somehow, it will! My story is much different; as I gave you a little of the story at the beginning of this handbook, I started off chasing the money while still in high school. As I got into the professional realm, I found myself wanting to work harder, to gain raises and promotions to justify raises. This is most likely because, just like most teenagers, I created early debt for myself that I needed to pay for. I also started a family early. Married by 21, I needed to begin to provide for a family early. Therefore; I began the "chase" that most adults start with. Chasing money instead of professional development and career growth. A very dangerous game. Don't get me wrong; I absolutely know that I may have struggled more to support my family at an early age if I had focused on only what I love instead of money at the time. But, looking back at it now; I firmly believe without any doubt that the money would have eventually caught up to what I love to do. How could it not? Besides; I worked hard and gave it my all at every position I worked.

Until you can use the "L" word; you may never find true career happiness. Finding it means finding a way to truly measure it. What makes you happy? In the work world? What will give you the security of feeling good about getting up every single day to go to a place, or log into a network to contribute to something significant? Answering those questions are a good way to start. We must take the time to accurately access our situation, wants and desires for a career to truly find the happiness we seek.

Chapter 3

Recognizing the Opportunity for Career Growth

What is career growth? How do you know when there is an opportunity for career growth? How do you properly attack that opportunity? What we have are many questions that require a sound decision and answer in order to be able to take the necessary next steps to explore career changes and growth. There are ways to determine if an opportunity for career growth has presented itself to you or is on the verge of being presented to you. Let's look at some factors of being able to recognize opportunities. We must be able to see and take advantage of the difference of internal and external opportunities. Going back to the initial questions; career growth is any opportunity to gain experience, development, or financial gain. We must be able to see these indicators when they arise. At times; getting the "dream job" is not always going to be on the table even if there is an opportunity for change. Gaining experience is very valuable. That experienced gained can be beneficial for the steps that come next to get that "dream job". Gaining professional experience can come in the form of a new position at your current organization, picking up additional duties within your current department, assisting partner departments in your organization, or volunteer/intern work outside of your organization. Each has significant value for getting to where you want to go in your career. Examining the different levels of professional experience align with knowing when an opportunity for career growth has been presented. Knowing the opportunity is coming is highly important. Think of being an out-fielder on a baseball team, you may spend most of the game watching the action, with not much to do. However; the key of your position is knowing that you must be ready, ready to get in position to be able to catch a pop-up or fly to cause an out for the opposing team.

Being ready to recognize career growth opportunities is just like being an outfielder. You may be in "job" mode, going through your daily routine of performing your position duties and making great progress daily, but you must always be ready to jump at an opportunity. In order to be ready to "jump", you must identify when the opportunity presents itself! Some ways to identify opportunity include being able to recognize opportunities, how they come, and when they come:

- Does the opportunity come from an existing colleague?
- Does the opportunity come from a recruiter or head-hunter?
- Does the opportunity come from a friend or associate?
- Is it in a form of a promotion?
- Is it a totally different world, outside opportunity that is taking a leap of faith?

Being ready to identify the opportunity when it comes saves you a lot of time when it comes to getting ready to decide to take a leap of faith and make a change in your career. When you can properly identify not only how you got the opportunity; but also if it is a legit opportunity and not just a run-around, or a waste of energy and resources, then you can switch your mind into the mode of getting ready to make a change in your career. Let's take some of the above-mentioned opportunities to further examine getting ready to take advantage of said opportunity. Looking at two of the avenues, first, a friend or associate has let you know about a potential job. There are some questions that you can ask yourself to determine if it is even worth it to go any further with pursuing the job, or stop, and say thanks and move on. Does the friend work for the company or department they are recommending? If so, how reliable is that friend? Do they have a good work record? Can they be trusted? Why are these questions important? You don't want to go and apply for a job that is recommended by a person who does not have good standing in the department or organization! Why? Because of preconceived notions. Unfortunately; many people believe that other people only hang around people that are just like them. I would have to say that I almost 90 percent agree with this notion. Be it, wrong or right. Therefore; if your friend let you know about a job where they work, and they are somewhat of the "class clown" What do you think are the chances of you getting the job? Especially, if they've taken the liberty to recommend you to their manager. You may waste a lot of time and effort on taking off work for the interview, attire, and preparing only to just be strung along and not get the job because the hiring manager is afraid you are much like your friend whom referred you. On the other end of this; if your friend is upstanding and has a good record and reputation at the organization or department, then you may have identified a great opportunity.

Let's now look at the recruiter/head-hunter opportunity. This is where you must be able to ask and answer unlimited questions, and research mightily. Some of the questioning must align with what you are good at, what you can become good at, and your overall reasoning for even considering the opportunity. When speaking with a recruiter, you want to establish that you have real value in the market and that you need to be a fit for the organization that they are recruiting for. It is good to ask the question of why this company needs an outside recruiter. Sure, most companies use outside recruiters in this era; but some companies may tend to lean on recruiters due to high turnover ratios because of a poor work environment. Finding out as much as you can about the work environment is important for being able to take the next steps in setting up a potential interview with the company. Going back to the initial questioning; a short list can be compiled to ask the recruiter regarding the company and your fit:

- Why are they trying to fill the position?
- How does my experience align with what they are looking for?
- What can I bring to the table to alleviate some pain points for my possible direct manager, and the company?

Those are some of the line of questioning that need to be asked. It is important to determine if this opportunity is more of a fire-drill/Band-Aid for a struggling company/department/manager. The last thing you want to do is begin negotiating and interviewing to go into a disaster situation. Attempt to get the recruiter to be honest about the situation before going far into the process. Quite honestly; it may be best to present yourself as only willing to take the "right match and situation". This will let the recruiter know that you mean business, and you are not just desperate for any opportunity that comes along.

After we've truly identified an absolute opportunity for real career growth, weeded through the avenues the opportunity has come from, and done any preliminary investigating and questioning as to why the opportunity has come along; then we can move into the jump. To attack an opportunity; we can start to rev up to taking real steps to get our mind ready to be prepared to move into a new challenge. Jumping at opportunities may seem a little too ambitious or non-loyal to some but think about it from the position of the owner of your company. His/her goal is to grow the business, at all cost. Why would you not be looking to grow your own brand? At any opportunity?

Hmmm! Now we make the connection! Career growth and recognizing the opportunities for it encompass more than just doing your daily duties and being loyal. Let's Segway into being ready to properly attack these opportunities when they come. In this current society, we have been empowered with instant contact, communication ability, and access. These come from the internet, and social media and Job sites. Having these tools gives us an opportunity to be ready for career growth advancements. Using social media, and job sites must be a strategic exercise. We cannot just apply to any and all jobs that we think can be the "dream job". Why? Let's discuss. Forming a strategy to becoming successful at professional development, staying relevant, and nabbing the "dream job" has to do with preparation. We will deep-dive into preparation in the next chapter, but for now, let's think about the pre-cursers for preparation regarding professional development and being competent enough to get the "dream job". As previously mentioned; we must be able to identify career growth, know when there is an opportunity for career growth, how to properly attack that opportunity, have the correct mindset to properly question the presented opportunity, and finally move into the attack mode to be able to present yourself as the correct candidate and match for the opportunity. Simply put, the opportunity must be right. Preparation leads to the right opportunities being presented. How? We gain knowledge in different roles in our professional journey, we gain experience; with experience comes confidence. Once you have ultimate confidence, then you are ready to prepare for any opportunity that comes. Either way, seeing the opportunity is barely enough. You must be able to take the leap. Preparing properly puts you in that position. How do we properly prepare? Let's go into the details.

Chapter 4   Preparing for the Big Day

Now that we can recognize and be ready to pounce on the presentment of career growth, let's discuss properly preparing when opportunity has engulfed us. A checklist must be compiled to ensure that you can be ready for the next steps of this new opportunity in your life now. We must be ready to be prepared in the following ways:

- Mentally
- Professional
- Academically
- Personable

Being mentally prepared encompasses quite a bit. I am sure that, for most; saying you are mentally prepared may simply lead us to believe that we must just be mentally strong. There is so much more to it than that! Being truly mentally prepared encompasses being focused, being disciplined, and strategic. Without those qualities, you may fall short of accomplishing goals such as reaching personal heights in your career. Your mentality goes a long way in carrying you through the ups and downs that come with navigating a career. Once you begin to master the strength of mental control, you can begin to prepare for more opportunity, and more growth. Focus is number one on the list for a reason. Being focused can be miss-interpreted as always being serious, or politically correct, or up-tight. Focus is far from these descriptions. Being able to focus means having clear vison, and being able to visualize every situation, responsibly thinking through decisions with extreme conscious and conviction. Becoming a more focused individual will lead to straighter paths in your life and get you ready for new challenges along the way. So, what does focus have to do with passing an interview for a job? Glad you asked! Remember, this section is targeting being mentally prepared for the job interview. Therefore; what could be more important for preparing for an interview than being focused?

Think about being in a situation where you truly dislike your job, and an interview finally comes along. Being focused means accepting that an opportunity has come, but you are still able to perform at a high level at your current position, you are still able to show respect to your manager and co-workers; even though you know there is a possibility you could be on the brink of leaving soon. Being focused means having the patience to be able to prepare for the opportunity and interview but move in the same manner visually to everyone around you, as if you are stuck in the same job and know it! This means, not making a public announcement about your upcoming interview. This means not feeling like you've already gotten the next job, even if you know for a fact that you're guaranteed to get the job. Nothing is final until it is final! Being focused in the wake of being offered a job interview, and the potential to progress in your career can mirror being a superhero. What is it that I mean by this? Take most superheroes; They walk around amongst ordinary people in ordinary clothing, living an ordinary life at day. This is you at your current job. Yet, at night; that superhero becomes just that! Throws on a cape and heads out to fight villains and save the world. This is you preparing for the interview and the new job. Be the bland everyday worker that you've always been, even though you know you're on the brink of saving the world tonight. Saving the world is conquering that job interview next Tuesday at 10am!

Good preparation takes much discipline! Being disciplined means sacrificing for the greater good. This is where we veer into the professional and academic preparation that we'll talk about a little later. Having good discipline regarding preparing for a job interview or an opportunity means missing the opportunity to go out after work for drinks, studying up on your field, or the field that you're interested in entering. Being disciplined means refreshing yourself on some of the stale tasks that you never get to do in your daily duties, but they are technically a part of your general description. Preparing in a disciplined manner for an upcoming job interview means putting extra effort into getting that hour and a half of additional sleep that you always seem to neglect. Why? Once you know you have a potential new opportunity, and you are going to have to be in a presentation mode soon; you need to get your body, appearance, and mind refreshed for the event. Trust me; there is nothing worse than going into an interview tired and sleepy, not focused, and stressed out due to lack of sleep. An interviewer will see it immediately. Of course; you may say, "well the interviewer will just simply see that I'm a hard worker and want me that much more, because they see that I am willing to put in all the extra hours to get the job done." Go ahead and sell that to yourself to believe. Also, go ahead and prepare the fudging that you will tell in the interview to convince the interviewer that you "put in all the extra hours"! Or, why not? As I previously said; the interviewer will see it from a mile away. A good interviewer will think, "I wonder why this individual needs to put in so much time and so many hours at their current job?" "Maybe they are not organized?" "Maybe they perform poorly; so, they work more hours to make up for poor performance?" Don't fall into the trap of fooling yourself into believing that you can convince someone that you work so many hours because you're so good. The good ones can cut down on their hours due to being very effective and disciplined at what they do!

If you can become focused and disciplined in your approach to preparing for a job interview, or an opportunity; you will then be able to become strategic in your approach. What does it mean to be strategic in an approach to preparing for an interview? This means finding ways to be ready to stand out. You are not the only candidate! You may be at the top of their list, in the middle, or barley hanging on for consideration. There is no way to know until the offer is made to you. Therefore; be strategic, research differently. Sure, the basics start with researching the job description; which we will go into further, later. But be ready to study up on the company's founder, the history of the company, the executive team, the mission, the reason the company exists. Know more than the average candidate. Far too many times, a candidate gets so wrapped up in just passing the interview, they become a robot. Don't be the robot! Be relaxed and conversational, but effective. A great way to do this is to be able to talk about the company specifically. We must remember; a good organization is not just looking at you to fill a job. A good organization is considering you to become a part of their family and grow with them and contribute significantly. Therefore; showing that you have some grasp of what the company is deeply rooted in and is trying to accomplish bodes well for your chances at passing the interview. Then you can move into preparing to answer all the tough questions that are position specific.

To prepare for a job professionally encompasses proper research. When researching a potential job due to being invited to a job interview; there are key elements to consider. The first thing to do is look at the job description. But let's pause for a moment and really think about that statement! Let's (Look at the Job description!) The emphasis on this cannot be taken lightly. As a former manager; I cannot count how many candidates I've interviewed whom did not really know what the job entailed. Sure, a position title can tell you what you will be doing, but the full job description gives vital details into what you need to do daily, weekly, or even monthly once you have the job. Looking at the job description must be simplified to simple math, or comparison lists. What I mean by this is literally look at each bullet point or sentence of the job description and create two lists. On the left; start a list of the bullets or sentences describing the job that you know 100% you fully understand and can do without any issues. The next list on the right side is a list of the remaining job duties that you are not fully confident you can do without extensive training; or either you are somewhat familiar with but need to investigate. Therefore; if you were going in for an interview for a job as an accountant, your list may look something like below:

Things I know	Possibly know, Not fully sure
Prepare asset, liability account entries	Compute taxes owed, prepare tax returns
Document financial account transactions	Substantiate financial transactions by auditing documents

Examine statements to ensure accuracy	Maintain accounting controls policies and procedures
Reconcile financial discrepancies by collecting and analyzing account information	
Verify, allocate, post and reconcile transactions	
Produce account reports and present their results	

Your lists may; and should be longer than the example above. It is important to outline every single task that comes with the job description. The lists above provide you with two solid advantages of going into an interview: 1st, you have identified every part of the job that you are confident, and good at. This will allow you to be able to be mentally refreshed on tasks that you already know, and be ready to speak freely, and at ease about the topics without any hiccups. You may ask; why should I acknowledge what I already know? Or what I am sure I can do in my sleep? Simple! There are not many jobs where the frequency of tasks is every-single-day, week in and week out.

Therefore; acknowledging the duties that you do well gives you an added advantage during the interview to present your wealth of knowledge when the opportunity presents itself. The second reason the lists provide you with an advantage during the interview, is that now you will take the actual time to research the tasks you don't know well. This allows you to discover any and all transferrable skills. Simply put, at first glance you may have 5 tasks that you don't feel confident about or feel that you have never done before. Yet, when you begin to research each task one-by-one; you will often find that you've done the task in some shape or form in your career, just not exactly how it is worded in the job description. This is due to every organization having its own language, or way of doing things. Though, a position such as an accountant is standard, you may find that; "OH! That is what they mean!" "I remember doing that!", or "I remember my manager doing that!" Now you have researched something you are not 100% confident in; but can articulate how to do it during an interview. See how that works?

There will be some tasks that even after researching them you just simply do not know what the task entails. Don't get worried, just be prepared to at least acknowledge that you know of it. That you've heard of it and can pick it up rather quickly. Unless the task you cannot identify is pretty much the actual job, chances are, you will be shown how "they do it" at that company anyway. It is also important to remember that if you are offered the job, there will be many reasons that hiring manager feels confident that you can do the job.

Being prepared academically can stand for many accomplishments in a professional career. Being prepared for opportunities does not just mean having a degree or degrees. Your work experience is the main academic preparation. Take pride in what you've accomplished so far in your journey. Own it! There is a reason you've been a front-line supervisor for 11 years! There is a reason you've been on that production line for 6 years! Own your experience! And be able to articulate that experience in very specific details. Just because your current or past titles don't have the glitter and glam on the name; does not mean what you've done isn't important or valuable. Be prepared to speak to that value, and how it transfers to future endeavors, and higher responsibility. Sure, if the position you are going to be interviewing for is specific to a certain field that took years of college and requires a specific degree to even be in the position to interview for it; by all means stay on track to deliver the scientific notes from your Masters and PHD coursework to prove your knowledge. Yet in most cases, even with advanced degrees, the interviewer still needs to see you articulate that you understand how to take your knowledge and break it down into basic everyday tasks, everyday human interaction, everyday courtesy and mutual respect. Therefore, I started this topic off with emphasis on being prepared academically as encompassing more than just higher education.

Just be yourself and show yourself! Period! There is no better way to display your true knowledge and talent than to do it as yourself! You cannot expect to be in an interview and spout off definitions of what the job entails. You must be able to have a relaxed conversation about how you fully understand what the job requires. You must be able to explain how you can deal with unexpected circumstances regarding what a normal job description would be. Also, an often-forgotten skill is adaptation to change. How can you take what you know, all the knowledge you have and use it to get through a tough unexpected situation on the job? How do you guide your team, or department through such a satiation? Therefore, preparing academically means so much more than just book smarts. To put it in very simple terms; we will use an old analogy often used in real-world discussions. Are you book smart? Or are you street smart? Do you have a little bit of both? You can probably tell that my preferred answer is the latter. Having both book smarts, and street smarts goes a long way, and this goes for any environment, neighborhood, or culture you grew up in! It also can be applied to preparing academically for a job interview or opportunity. Embrace your formal education! But, also embrace your hard-working experience and grind ability that had nothing to do with formal education! Own both! Present both!

Being personable includes quite a bit when nailing the interview experience. First, there is being polite and direct with every conversation, email, phone call. It is highly important to present yourself well to potential managers, organizations, and recruiters. Being personable starts with the initial email or phone call. Respond in a timely manner, or take the call, if you can. If you've already decided that it is time to make a change in your career; then why would you not be prepared to take a call from a recruiter or respond to an email. Of course, this does not mean begin to be disrespectful to your current employer, manager, or role. But, make the time to respond in a timely manner to recruiters, if you are indeed "open for business"!

When you do respond to that email, or take that call, or call back; show that you're truly interested. Let the recruiter know that you are ready to make a move, but not for anything! Make it clear in the nicest, most honest way that you know you're worth, and are looking for the right fit. Being able to inform a recruiter that it is important to you that the next opportunity has to be the right fit for not only you, but for the employer gives you some points towards winning the interview, before the interview is even offered. From my experience, this works! It's genuine or feels genuine. What it does is comport a feeling of morality to the recruiter. Far too many times, a candidate has the resume, gets through the interview, but is simply not a fit. Expressing the importance of fit is a great way to get the recruiter leaning in your favor right away. An absolute way to display personable traits at the introduction of the process.

Having flexibility is also very important. Let's say you got an interview scheduled for Tuesday morning. The interview goes extremely well.

Later that afternoon, you get a call-back from the H.R department expressing that the interviewer loved your personality and thinks that you're a fit but would like you to have a follow up interview with another team member, or senior management tomorrow! Well, more than likely, you've either taken the day off for the interview, left early, or went to work late at your current job. What do you do? You make the interview tomorrow! But how? You make it happen tomorrow! Why should you bend over backwards for a job that may not be yours? Let's stop and think about the circumstance here. If the human resources representative calls you and asks you to do a quick turnaround, they know you will likely have to pull strings to make it happen. No, they are not trying to test you. The most likely reasoning is that they were blown away by your self-presentation and want to quickly get you in front of true decision makers to close the deal.

Therefore; make it happen!

Prospective organizations are not calling the "blah candidates" for a quick turnaround interview tomorrow! Trust me! They are hoping to eliminate, and politely be able to turn down the "blah candidates; as soon as you accept their offer the day after!

Chapter 5 — During the Interview

Taking all the preparing into account that we've just discussed; we've prepared accordingly, and now we can discuss moving into the actual interview marathon. During the interview process, we must take everything that makes us what we are, and a bit more to be able to competently be able to perform during the marathon. I like to call this exercise "Surviving". I know, I know! That may seem a little harsh or let the thought of making interviews difficult begin to creep into the mind. But it is exactly the opposite. Why? How? There is absolutely nothing to ever be afraid of or nervous when it comes to interviewing! Period! Let's really let that sink in again and repeat it to make sure that we fully understand why we are here right now.

There is absolutely nothing to ever be afraid of or nervous when it comes to interviewing! Period!

Let's not make a mistake to why this handbook was written. Nor make any mistake as to why you are sitting reading this handbook! Of course, this handbook contains many solid references, and tips to get you through recognizing, preparing, and getting through interviews, but let's understand that I want to make sure that I can instill a sense of confidence in every single individual that reads this handbook that You Can Conquer Any Interview! It is really that simple. Continue reading, then combine it with what you've read in this handbook already, in addition to your knowledge that you already have, and voila! Any interview can be survived!

Diving in to being amid the interview process begins now. We can start off first by determining if to be either the aggressor or the defender. Being the aggressor means that you've covered everything we've discussed previously, and you are one hundred percent sure that you have mastered everything. You know why you're looking for a new opportunity. You've hammered down the "Five Deciders". You've positively recognized a true potential for career growth. You've also taken the proper amount of time to prepare, mentally, professionally, academically, and personably. Well, now you can go into that interview as the aggressor; the SME (subject matter expert) on all topics. Your confidence should be at top level if you've done all the prior prep-work. You can approach the interviewer with extreme intelligence and present to them in a way that absolutely blows them away. But let's not get carried away here. We still need to remain humble in measures. Speaking of humbleness; I will dive into that a little more later, when I cover the final stage of "Mastering Your Interview Experience." But to get into it a bit, remember a common theme of this handbook is to approach an interview and an interviewer in a relaxed, conversational tone and manner. Absolutely be aggressive in how you answer the questions; meaning leaving no doubt that you are prepared and understand every question that comes your way. Yet, be calm, and gradually take control of the interview. Express yourself clearly and concisely. Force the interviewer to understand that you've prepared for this, not just in the week prior; but as a professional with your experience!

One of the best things one can do in an interview is make an interviewer run out of job specific questions. Trust me; in my experience of interviewing candidates as a manager; I've always had a list of questions for the candidate, weather I wrote them down or recited them from memory. It was rare but did happen a few times that I exhausted all my questions that were job specific. Guess what was next? You bet, getting to really know the person interviewing for the position; and not the person in front of me that is nervous, or the person that prepared specifically for my job-related questions. This is when you bridge the gap between being a robot - super prepared interviewee; to becoming the picture of an ideal candidate that fits the organizational culture. This is when the interviewer starts to see some of themselves in you or relate to you more. Therefore; having to be in the aggressor role is good, because it gives you an opportunity to grab control of that interview, sooner than later.

There will be times you need to be the defender. What is it that I mean by being a defender in an interview? Relax! No one is going to or should slander you; drill you like a criminal in an interview. Though; there will be situations in which the line of questioning gets a bit difficult. There are varying reasons why an interviewer will come off as drilling you a little. Some of those reasons may be:

- The interviewer does not really know what the job entails
    - Therefore, they have researched some job specific questions that may not necessarily apply, or are outdated

- The interviewer does not trust what they see on your resume
- The interviewer has some pre-conceived notion of who you are prior to meeting you

No matter the reason; one of the three above, or some other reason, you may have to shift into defender mode on an interview. To do this means to back up your resume. It goes back to being able to present your preparedness. Speak academically, speak of that professional experience you have, be personable while you explain that not only do you know exactly what the job requires; you can add value that may not be there. Speak of how you improved processes, procedures, became an asset to a department. Being the defender is much like being on trial, you are there to dispute any notion that you are not the best candidate! And you'll fight to the end! "Of that interview", "With a confident presentation of your knowledge and skills" Then they will have no choice but to seriously consider you for the job!

Weather you find yourself becoming the aggressor or the defender during an interview; there are two qualities you must always exude to get you through the "During" part of an interview. Those two qualities are; controlling your emotion and displaying confidence without arrogance. Ah; the emotion and confidence qualities. Think about emotion for a moment, since we discussed potentially being an aggressor, we must also check our ego at the door. This means absolutely speaking with great confidence about yourself, your work history, your knowledge, your experiences throughout your career, or education. Yet, let it flow naturally, and calmly. Don't over-emphasize your greatness. Your greatness should shine through easily with your conversation. Doesn't matter if you're the aggressor or defender in the interview; you should exude extreme confidence, without arrogance. Keep some relevance of humble in your conversation, while continuing to make it clear that you are made for this position, this challenge! Make the interviewer understand that you have value, and you know your value. Never let an interviewer miss-interpret that you don't know your value. This is where the confidence comes in. but, use your knowledge and experience to explain why you are so valuable. This is where confidence without arrogance takes the stage.

I briefly spoke about when the opportunity comes to take control. This is what I have dubbed "The Window" There is always going to be a moment in an interview when the interviewer will give you control of the session. It may be a question; it may be a comment they make. In some cases, the interviewer will not even know they are opening that window. Alas! DO NOT MISS THE OPPORTUNITY TO CLIMB THORUGH THAT WINDOW AND OWN THE INTERVIEW FROM THAT POINT ON!

But how do we know when the "Window" has been cracked? Let's get into it! Some ways to know when to take over an interview include:

- The interviewer runs out of job specific questions
- The interviewer asks you a question that requires you to give an anecdote
- You have a few moments of silence during the interview
- The interviewer cannot contain the fact that they've bought in to who you are and what you can bring

These are some examples of seeing and capturing the "Window" to take over the interview. This is when you overwhelm the interviewer with your wit, charm, knowledge, and expertise to clamp down the position before you leave that room. This now becomes the survival section of the interview. Basically, don't mess it up! You've almost won the battle!

So, you're in this interview and you've identified if you should be the aggressor or defender and acted accordingly, you've exuded confidence without arrogance, and remained humble, gotten through the line of job specific questioning. What now? Try to wrap it up neatly and get to know the organization from the view of the interviewer. This is the beginning stage of the survival portion of the interview. Let's call it survival prep. I know, I know! How can you possibly know from an interviewer's view? Well, let me explain. You must Identifying if the organization is even for you during the interview. Do this by looking for indicators that the organization may be unstable and decide if you are better off where you currently work. Yes, even during the interview that is going well, there is still a possibility that you won't want to accept the job or feel it is a fit for you:

- Are there a lot of new/short tenured employees? Does not hurt to ask, unless this is a start-up, and it has been made perfectly clear that they want you to be a part of this start-up
- Does the hiring manager lack a sense of direction for the company or department? Ask them about the

direction they are headed, and how they envision you getting them there
- Ask about time-off, remote working ability – See if they stress about the question. This may indicate that the environment may not be for you due to being unstable

Besides everything we just discussed, we must also identify if the interviewer is not interested or harassing. Unfortunately; in some hiring processes, the candidate has almost been 95% identified. You may say, then why did they bring me in? Well, your interview may have already been scheduled with a cloud of candidates, and someone already blew them away. But they do want to see if you can, in their view, beat out that another candidate. In some cases, the preferred candidate may be internal, but their policy may be to bring in so many candidates. Either way, some interviewers lack professionalism in these situations. Therefore; they may be very aggressive, or try to be intimidating, because they already know they don't intent to hire you. We must be able to see this and switch our mind into "get out" mode. What is "get out" mode? It's staying professional, even if the interviewer is not, but begin to give short-to-the point answers to prepare to end the interview. Staying calm is key, make up in your mind that it is time to move on from this potential opportunity. Besides, if the interviewer is being harassing; you shouldn't want to work for this organization anyway! This may seem hasty, but you do not want to waste any more time, if you've identified that the interviewer does not really want you, or like you. And even if you could turn them and make it through this interview to the next stage; do you really want to work for an organization that allows such behavior? Though it is not uniform in all organizations, an H.R. professional or manager, should have had some form of compliance training to be able to stay professional and not; "show their hand" in the interview, be-it positive or negative. Of course, there will be moments when you absolutely hit a "home-run" with the interviewer rather quickly, and they "just have to have" you. But a negative, harassing interviewer must be handled properly for the professional exit. But, let's say that we've done every part of the "during" exercise in this interview; and the interviewer is not a harassing jerk, and the organization seems to be a fit for you. Let's back-track a little bit as we move forward to discuss the surviving skills needed in the "During" portion of the interview.

Chapter 6   Surviving

To continue the "during" process of the interview and move into the survival section of the interview gradually; we can apply the following survival methods. Transferrable skills, presentation, and competence of question answering. To be able to come out of an interview on the successful end, knowing that you've just set the interviewer back on their heels is a great feeling. How do you accomplish this feat? Well, we've covered quite a bit into how to do just that, but now let's get into the room. Let's visualize that we are sitting in that room right now in front of the interviewer, ready to survive this challenge, set them back on their heels, and walk out knowing that we will be getting a great offer very soon! As most interviews go; a line of questioning will more than likely kick-off the process. This is where most people fail at interviews. Whether it is from being nervous or not being prepared; a lot of very qualified individuals just cannot get through the line of questioning smoothly. As there are many interview questions, and they all vary depending on the nature of the job, the field or sector of business; we will not go through a question – and how to answer exercise. Yet I do want to address some of the basic, high-level run-of-the-mill questions that will generally pop up at just about any interview. We must remember that, as mentioned throughout this handbook; an interview is a conversation and should be viewed as such. There is no reason to have anxiety about answering basic questions in an interview.

To begin discussing how to answer the basic interview questions, let's remember that the most important aspect to do is be honest about yourself and every answer. It makes no sense to be dis-honest and try to fool the interviewer. This will more than likely lead to you not getting the job, or finding a way to get the job, only to be short tenured because the manager eventually finds out that you're a hoax. Some of the typical questions you will find at every job interview include:

- ✓ Name your strengths

So, how do we answer the question of, name our strengths? With the intention of being honest, simply explain what you do, and have done well in your career and roles. This is not an opportunity to become arrogant and brag about yourself, it is an opportunity to speak of your value to an organization, and previous roles. Talk about examples when you had to step up outside of what your job required. Speak in detail about previous job reviews, and compliments that you've received from management and co-workers, customers or employees. Keep in mind, your strengths should note something that set you apart from previous co-workers. I've found that in my own interview experiences, and when interviewing candidates, the most impressive answers to this question involved explaining times when you performed a beneficial role, or task that had nothing to do with your daily job duties. This is where you'll find your meat for this answer. As you prepare for your next interview, remember to build a list of memory about those times that you step outside the box, and went above and beyond to help your department or manager. These are true strengths. Be able to explain these situations, and word them as a strength of yours during the interview. To be more specific and provide an example; I'll give you one of my strength answers to use to build your own. I remember a time when I worked in a bank operations unit, and our partner unit was severely understaffed for a shift. That partner unit was a unit I previously worked with; as I had been promoted to manage this new unit. Seeing that unit was so understaffed, and knowing that I had the knowledge to perform their tasks; I appointed a member of my staff to run my unit for the day; then I went over to manage and help the partner unit make it through the shift and meet deadlines. Thus, effectively enabling two production units to complete bank activities for the day. This is a specific example of the strength of Initiative. My anecdote explains the strength of initiative in detail. This is how the strengths questions should be handled. Give your noun, then explain it with detail. It is up to you how many strengths you name. 2 -3 is a good measure.

- ✓ Name your weaknesses

Okay! The weakness questions. No one likes this question because no one feels they have any weaknesses. Yet this is a question that will come up during an interview. We must be prepared to answer this question, like it or not. We can keep this one very simple and to the point. Explaining your weaknesses should be based on how you've overcome those weaknesses, or plan to overcome those weaknesses. The first rule of answering this question is to never-ever point out failures or shot-comings you've experienced at work or in certain work situations. It's just not a good idea. It may make you appear to come off incompetent or dwelling on the negative, or a mope. Instead; speak of the unknown regarding your career and experience. A good example is to turn this answer into a testament of goals that you intend to accomplish to better your own career value, and possibly add more value to their company with you as an employee. A specific example is to say, "I feel that I am extremely good at accounting, but I am studying for the CPA, so one of my weaknesses is not yet having that CPA under my belt" What you've done is given the interviewer a look into the fact that you're a person who sees weaknesses as temporary, and are prepared to eliminate those weaknesses. To be more general; I've often answered this question in a very broad manner and have been successful with the response from the interviewer. I've answered; "I would say my weakness is anything that I don't yet know, but anything I don't know, I intend to study, work hard and learn to better myself!" Again, this is a very effective way to answer the question of weakness, without pointing out that you could potentially be incompetent at anything. In review, a weakness should be termed as the unknown when answering this question during an interview.

- ✓ What are your short and long-term career goals?

Speaking about your goals. This should be very easy to do. First, you are sitting in the interview because you recently had a short-term goal to change jobs. You're almost there. Again, stay honest when answering this question as well. When answering this question, you don't want to start to read off a long book at every-single thing you want to accomplish in your life and career. What you want to do here is get specific with anything that you plan or have planned to do that is relatable to the position you are interviewing for, or the company itself. Explain how you plan to get your MBA, or that certificate for technology. Talk about how a short-term goal of yours includes learning this position if you're the candidate chosen, because you know it will help you attain a different career goal of yours in the future. What this does is tell the interviewer that you feel like you're a match for the organization, and you believe that in the role, you will be able to enhance not only your own level of professional development, but in turn be able to contribute significantly to the organization in the future. Very effective!

- ✓ Speak about a challenging work experience

A Challenging work experience explanation can vary depending on what you've been through, the type of work you've done, and the types of organizations you've worked for. This is, in my opinion the first Trick Question!

Why do I consider this a trick question? I say this because when I interviewed candidates, this is when I wanted to see if the individual was a dweller of negative, held grudges, or was a deflector of blame. See where I'm going with this? This question is designed to bring out the worst in you, or at least your worst quality if you like to complain about other short-comings and weaknesses. What we must understand is, that at every job, there are people and situations that you just simply did not like. Whether or not you contributed to whatever the issue was at the time; an interview is not the arena to go on and on complaining about a co-worker, manager, or situation that upset you. Use this question and answer to explain a challenge that impeded work progress, or meeting deadlines, and how you, and your manager and co-workers handled the situation and recovered from catastrophe. Like the strengths question, this is an opportunity to explain how you contributed to problem solving and issue resolution in a department or organization. No rants here! Please!

- ✓ What is your view on team and team related environment at work?

The good-ole teamwork environment question. As we move further into our modern technology driven society with everyone carrying around a lap-top to have the ability to work remotely; the old idea of team environments has changed significantly. But it has not gone away by the slightest. Our newfound independence at work has led a lot of us to believe that we don't want to be a part of a team or team environment. Far from the truth! You and I both know this isn't true. Therefore, make sure you can express this in an interview. Be able to explain some examples of how you worked within the framework of a team and excelled. Give examples of times when a team environment was not going as expected, and what you did to corral the team to get the task completed successfully. Being able to communicate how you fit in a team and would be able to co-exist with team members that don't quite cooperate is a good way to answer this question.

Above are 5 of the most common run-of-the-mill interview questions that we will find during an interview. Your interview experience will vary depending on the organization, the field of work, or the actual interviewers personal experience at interviewing, but these basic questions seem to follow all walks of life. Now that we've went through the exercise of how to answer these questions, let's remember the key elements of an interview and how to be successful at an interview: Be honest, and keep the interview conversational! As we move forward into technological advancements, real-world experience driving hires, and organizations looking to hire individuals as more of a partnership, than a boss-employee relationship; we should see these basic questions disappear more and more in interviews. But, as they do remain in some of the more formal interview settings, it's good that we've covered them.

Outside of the questioning that will take place during an interview, and the proper way to answer those questions; we must also be mindful and prepared in other ways. Our overall presentation is highly important and must be given the proper amount of attention. Your appearance, disposition, and self-awareness of your presentation are just as important as being able to properly and correctly answer questions during an interview. With presentation, the first aspect must be appearance. One must be sure to always look their best for a job interview.

This means always wearing a nice suit, or a nice button up shirt with a tie or nice blouse. Even if you do not coordinate an entire suit, at least always wear the shirt with tie, nice blouse and a nice neat jacket to compliment the shirt. Interviews are not a business casual event! Let's repeat that one more time; Interviews are not a business casual event! This is very important! Why? Appearance is the first thing an interviewer sees when they meet you. Including nice attire; we must always be well-kempt, clean shaven, hair properly dressed, and hygiene optimal. Of course, there are instances where you may already know the interviewer and company; the interview scheduler may even tell you, "There is no need to wear a suit". Do it anyway! Trust me! Your appearance shows that you are serious about this opportunity, even if the suit is not required. For example, I interviewed two candidates in one day for a position. One candidate worked very early hours, and asked for mid-morning interview, as they would leave work early that day for the interview. The other candidate worked afternoons and opted for an early morning interview.

To give you an idea of how appearance can steer an interviewer the wrong way before they even hear your conversation about why you're the right candidate for the job; let me explain what happened with these two candidates. The candidate that worked afternoons was a young lady, and believe it or not, she came to the interview with a ponytail, and stretch pants and a casual shirt. Immediately I was thrown by her appearance, but I figured, let me conduct the interview as normal and not dwell on her appearance, due to the fact that her resume was impeccable, and her work history matched up with the position I wanted to fill. However, there was another problem; this lady had a huge bag, kind of a duffle bag/big purse looking bad, and it looked packed. At this point, she lost me, I was totally distracted, not only because of her appearance, but also because of this huge bag! I was thinking to myself, "If she didn't take the time to dress up, then what could possibly be in that huge bag?" I was done with the interview before it started. To be honest, I am not sure if I even went through my total line of questioning, due to being so distracted. The afternoon interview was quite impressive to say the least. This candidate was a young male, that worked all morning on his shift and rushed over to do the interview after leaving work early. However, he was clean shaven, well suited, and had impeccable hygiene upon arrival for the interview. He was also early and waiting in the lobby for me when I arrived to pick him up. See the difference here? The reason appearance is so important for an interview, is because as a candidate trying to prove you can fit; there is enough stacked against you form the start, beginning with other candidates, so why give an interviewer anything else to count a strike against you?

Our disposition is highly important, just like appearance. We want to come off as approachable and inviting, no guards up. To be more specific, I'll use myself as an example. People that know me personally feel that I am very serious, too serious at times. Not introverted, but a bit stand-offish in different situations. Some may even tell you that I'm just plain mean or have a mean – "don't approach me" look on my face at times. But in an interview, I am sunny, relaxed, approachable, smiling, and inviting. This is just the way I approach an interview, and interviewer. I can change my disposition for the purpose of the interview. Let's not confuse what I am able to do with being fake or phony. I just simply understand that, even though I am a very serious minded individual, the interviewer may interpret that disposition wrong, and it could potentially ruin the interview for me. Therefore; I adjust for the cause. Having a negative or nonexcited disposition on an interview can leave you in a bad spot, and not getting the job. This is because the interviewer may feel as if you are just too mean to fit into their organizational culture, or you are just going through the motions on this interview for whatever reason, but do not really want to join the organization.

Stay aware of your presentation, and disposition throughout the interview process. What does this mean? Pay attention to if you are smiling or not, are you making eye contact? Are you slouching in your chair? Is your head up? Are speaking clearly, and loud enough without yelling? All of this is something that should be a self-check throughout the interview. I know; you are thinking, "how can I do all of this and still answer questions and give my experience history?" Practice makes perfect! Everything I just mentioned, and all advice preceding in previous chapters is a part of being able to comfortably communicate in a conversational manner. If you cannot do this; practice it. Trust me! You can get to this level. Practice in a mirror, or with your significant other, or friend. Practice if you feel you can't be comfortable on an interview and pay attention to your presentation, disposition, while still being able to answer question and be natural.

There will come a point in the interview where a couple things will happen. The interviewer's line of questioning will run out, you will have answered everything correctly, and the interview is just about to hit the wrapping up stages. This is when you can take the opportunity to try and get a little personal with the interviewer. What is it that I mean by this? Speak about some of your personal life, such as where you grew up, what you like to eat, or your family. You just may strike a chord with the interviewer and get them to open a bit and relax even more than they already have. Of course, every interview and interviewer will not present a chance to do this, but if you see it, you must pounce! If you see an opportunity to do this; get personal, and successfully do it, there is a very high chance that interviewer will be leaving your session telling the H.R. department, "I've found the person!" Once you've determined if it is appropriate to get personal or not, you will enter the closing stages of the interview. At this point, you may have possibly read if the interviewer likes you or not, and possibly even be able to tell if you've gotten them to lean towards picking you for the position. This is where you keep your composure, finish out the interview process and don't mess it up!

What is it that I speak of when I say, "don't mess it up"? Let the interview wind down naturally. You may even be able to give the reins back to the interviewer at this point, if you were earlier able to take control of the interview during the "window". But don't mess things up. Don't unwind all the good you've accomplished at this point. Close out the interview smoothly and naturally. Ask closing questions such as; What is the timeline of deciding on the position? Speak enthusiastic about the potential to join the team. Speak appreciative and grateful for the opportunity to even interview. Do all of this as you exit, with a great smile and demeanor to close out what was a successful interview process. This will leave even more of an impression on the interviewer. That interviewer will, "have to have you" at this point.

Chapter 7 You got the Job!

Well, well, well! They want you! You blew the interviewer away! Now your staring at an offer sheet wondering if the salary is enough, or if you should negotiate a little more? What's next? First is deciding if you like the offer, and reflecting on the interviewer, the environment as you walked into the office for the interview, and the whole process from beginning to end. If you can answer yes to; "it was a very pleasant experience to interview with this organization" then you will more than likely be accepting the offer. Now you will be going back into some of the initial "Five Deciders" as we move into the acceptance of the position phase of the process. Look at the offer sheet, is the salary what you expected? If it is, you're good. If not, then its time to think about how to negotiate what you want. You should always ask for more than you want in a negotiation. Why? Because it is a negotiation. The hiring company will try to, in most cases, get you at a premium price. This is where recognizing your value and talents come into play. Know your worth. If the salary on the offer letter is not enough, ask for more! More than you really want so that your new salary can fall comfortably into a space that was worth all the stressful interviewing process you just went through.

Do not be afraid to ask for more or negotiate. Why? We must keep in mind that since you got an offer letter, you have effectively beat out and eliminated who knows how many other candidates. They want you now! Make sure they pay you now! In my experience, the average Human resources department or hiring manager should be expecting a counteroffer at a very high percentage of the time. Unless they already know they've offered over market value to get you. Negotiating brings back in the aspect of research as well. First, you should have never been going for a job that you are not aware of the "going pay rate" for the position. All of this should be researched ahead of even applying. But, if you did not back then, do it now, with the offer letter in hand. Most job sites have a section where they estimate a salary nationwide for specific titles. Look for your title and decide on if you need to negotiate.

Look at the offer letter, see if it describes the position that you're offered in any way, or just lists the position name. Make sure the position name is exactly what you thought it would be, and what you interviewed for. I've seen cases when the position on the offer letter is slightly named different than what was applied for. This could be an honest mistake on the H.R department of the hiring company, or on purpose. Make sure you are about to take the position you intended to take. If it is different, you will need to contact the human resources department for an explanation. Don't be afraid to question everything at this point. You are the one making a change that will likely affect your entire life. Lastly, think about your potential new commute, and if it is indeed better than what you are doing now. It most likely is, unless this whole process was strictly a money grab for you. Your offer letter will most likely state the office you will report to as well. Make sure it aligns with what was discussed. Think back to the interview, and make sure that you can deal with any aspect mentioned by the interviewer that you did not quite like but played off a good disposition as to not mess up the interview. Are these one or two things a deal breaker? Make sure you can adjust, because its rare that every single aspect of an organization is perfect, and a good interviewer would have covered what they thought would be sticking points with you based on your work history. Now send back the acceptance and let's get started in our new adventure!

Chapter 8 — Life After

So now that you've aced the interview, and gotten the job, you learn that this is exactly the type of environment, and situation that you've always wanted. You've found career eutopia! Therefore; you're set! No need to ever think about looking again because you can see yourself retiring here. Wrong!

Get Ready to Perform! Period! Be ready to show your new employer why they chose you. You bragged during the initial discussion on the phone with the human resources representative or the recruiter, you bragged in the interview, you made these group of people believe that you are the perfect match for their open position and organizational culture. Now it's time to put up or shut up! We must display all the qualities we boasted about in that interview we mastered. If not? You may find yourself back in the interview cycle rather quickly. This is not what we want for obvious reasons. Sure, no one is hanging around jobs for 30-40 years anymore as our parents and grandparents did before but changing jobs every couple month's is not a good idea at all! Red flags will be everywhere, and eventually the emails, and calls from recruiters will dry up and disappear. Therefore; be ready to get going and perform. Remember all the research and preparation you did to get ready for this interview? You thought you were done, didn't you? No way! Now that you have the job, leading up to the start date, look over the job description again, look at it again, and really evaluate every-single task that is laid out in the description. Prepare again, this means researching the company, the field and looking up definitions of any tasks that you are not 100% comfortable performing with little-to-no training. This is important, because with every job, you will have some training, and a get-to-know phase. You may be able to take some valuable notes during your first couple days, maybe even weeks. Eventually you will be left to fly on your own. Therefore, we must research and fully understand those tasks that we didn't prior to taking this job. Basically, have a general understanding of everything in the job description. I know, no-one is an ace at everything they have listed on the description. You will soon find that there are even more tasks that the employer failed to mention or list on the description. The employer knows this, they hired you for the 1-5 things that they know you can rock-and-roll with right out of the gate. Your talent and what you excel at already is what got you here but be prepared to have knowledge of the tasks you are not fully comfortable with and be ready to soak up any training like a sponge.

Understand levels of training in your new role. What I mean by this is your level of experience will determine how much training you receive in your new role. Therefore, there is a theme in this handbook about being honest in the interview process, being conversational, and staying true to yourself and your real value. Levels of training will be based on your experience and pay level as such:

- Entry level to mid experience and salary: Training sessions, possibly side-by-side or class
- Mid to semi high level experience and salary: Some training, or shown how to do the tasks, and then left to perform. Possibly some self-training videos or classes
- High level experience and salary: You are expected to be a SME (Subject matter expert) – Little to no training. Figure everything out with just guidance on "how it is done" in that organization

Of course, the above levels are harsh and to the point, and some organizations may have adopted a vigorous training plan, no matter the level of hire. But in most cases, if your bought in at a high level and high salary, you are going to be looked to come in with an impact, make improvements, and recommendations for improvements, therefore, training will be minimal. You'll have to be ready to rock-and-roll. Entry level to mid-level can expect training and maybe even some step-by-step walk throughs. But that research and preparing you did leading up to your start date should have you ready to conquer anything that you've previously had limited experience with.

Now a couple weeks have passed, and you are starting to feel good about your decision. The employer and manager, and team are beginning to feel good about you being an addition to the team. Let's start thinking about retirement from this great situation. Nope! This is the point we begin to pick back up on professional development. Start to think of ways to continually improve yourself. This could mean many things. Sure, this may be the place you want to wrap up a career with. You may have found your career utopia. Still begin the process of improving yourself professionally. Even if it means looking for ways to take on more at this new company. Look into if they offer development courses at the company. Start looking into ways to gain more responsibility and experience. Branch off into helping others on the team. Trust me; it will pay off for you with this company in the long run. Let's say this new job is okay, not bad, but not the dream job. Basically, you know that there will be another company after this. In that case work hard and take on new responsibility, but start your professional development outside of the job, on your own time. Or pick up where you left off with your own professional development before you took this role. Not finding the perfect job after going through the stressful interview process is okay. It happens! But stay composed, don't talk about your dislikes about the new company at all, at least at work. And start the preparation for a new search again, quietly and composed. Either way, the point is to stay relevant in the market.

Staying relevant means to always keep all your job board profiles up to date. Always stay looking for opportunity even if you don't plan to apply for anything. I think it is always good to look at job postings to see what is out there, what type of money titles are getting, and what type of roles companies are trying to fill. There isn't even anything wrong with speaking with a recruiter here and there, or even interviewing for another position. I would advise that if you really like what you're doing, and like the company your work for, keep your job board profiles up to date. Why? You want to stay relevant in the market. When you're happy with your job, it just simply becomes a different conversation with a recruiter for a potential job. Believe it or not, now you've become empowered and can speak boldly about salary requirements, right out of the gate in a conversation with a recruiter; because your happy in your current role. If they really want to bring you in for a discussion, or possibly an interview, you can turn them down politely, or this is where you can really obtain very high salaries. But, be careful about this, as we now know that higher salaries may put you in a zone that you may not be comfortable in. And if you really like what you're doing and the company, why entertain it?

Chapter 9 — Conclusion

Now that we've gone through all possible roads regarding the interview process; you should feel better prepared to go into any interview and own it! Its all about knowing when you've found your sweet spot within the interview. It's about knowing your own comfort level to hold a relaxed conversation that is filled with important facts about you. About your experience. About your competency, and your confidence to get the job done. Acing an interview is not a con game. Sure, there are fields and sectors of professionalism where people simply study to pass an interview, studying specific questions that are very technical to fool the interviewer into thinking they know the job and the requirements well. What you will find in situations such as this are people who get a job, and it is short-lived. Then it is on to the next opportunity or you'll find failing unorganized organizations that are doomed anyway because the organization does not take the time to invest in proper recruiters, human resources staff who know how to interview and hire the right candidates.

This handbook has outlined the steps and stages to see an opportunity, attack an opportunity, prepare for the opportunity, and survive the interview process that comes with that opportunity. Far too many times, I hear people tell me that they get so nervous when it is time to interview for a job; be it, internal with their current organization or externally for a new opportunity. Why? Preparation is not up to par. This handbook shows that preparation starts far before we apply for a job, or even before we get invited to an interview. We must switch our mind state to thinking about professional development, even when we are happy in our current roles. Always staying prepared to jump on an opportunity. This way, we can always avoid the nervousness that comes with trying to convince someone you are the right candidate for a role. Once we own our value, we win! Owning our value means recognizing what we are capable of. What we can achieve! As mentioned throughout the handbook, we do this by preparing mentally, professional, academically and personable. When we prepare in each of these ways, it gives us an opportunity to project positively, speak confidently without arrogance, and hold a relaxed conversation with the interviewer.

All these traits set us up to be able to properly ask and answer any questions during an interview. It also gives us an opportunity to show the interviewer that we are indeed a fit for their organization. This is the whole purpose of the interview. Keeping this in mind, we can properly take control of an interview and let the interviewer know that they are sitting in front of a person with a wealth of talent that is able to project that talent into various roles to be beneficial to any organization. If you notice a theme in this handbook, you will see that we have basically gone through a cycle. We started with the question of why are we even looking? To deciding if we should make a move and determining if we've prepared for a move. Once we moved into recognizing if we have an opportunity for career growth, we attack an opportunity with the confidence and knowledge that we've built up over a career-long exercise. After we've secured a new opportunity, our focus shifts to performing, and staying relevant. Well, to round everything up into a neat bundle, we can step back and notice that performing at a high level at our job, and staying relevant in the market, accomplishes something very important for us. It gives us the chance to see new opportunities as they come, question if we should even look at the opportunity, decide if we should make a move, and determining if we've prepared for a move. As the cycle starts over, we can clearly see if we have an opportunity for career growth, and again attack that opportunity!

Made in the USA
Coppell, TX
21 February 2020